D0596266

To

From

Date

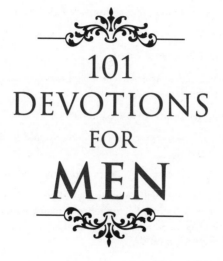

101
DEVOTIONS
FOR
MEN

Christian art gifts®

Visit Christian Art Gifts, Inc. at www.christianartgifts.com

101 Devotions for Men

Published by Christian Art Gifts, Inc.

Adapted from *Divine Moments for Men: Everyday Inspiration from God's Word*

First printing by Tyndale House Publishers

Questions and notes copyright © 2008 by Ronald A. Beers. All rights reserved.

Managing editors: Ronald A. Beers and Amy E. Mason

Contributing writers: V. Gilbert Beers, Rebecca J. Beers, Brian R. Coffey, Jonathan Farrar, Jeffrey Frasier, Jonathan Gray, Shawn A. Harrison, Sandy Hull, Rhonda K. O'Brien, Douglas J. Rumford, Linda Taylor

Edited by Michal Needham

Designed by Christian Art Gifts

Cover and interior images used under license from Shutterstock.com

Scripture quotations are taken from the *Holy Bible*, New Living Translation, copyright © 1996, 2004. Used by permission of Tyndale House Publishers, Carol Stream, Illinois 60188. All rights reserved.

Printed in China

ISBN 978-1-4321-3495-2 (Faux Leather)
ISBN 978-1-77637-115-0 (Hardcover)

22 23 24 25 26 27 28 29 30 31 – 10 9 8 7 6 5 4 3 2 1

Be on GUARD. Stand firm in the FAITH. Be COURAGEOUS. Be STRONG.

1 Corinthians 16:13

GODLY AMBITION

Ambition can be compared to fire—both have the potential to be powerfully productive or terribly destructive. When fire is kept in a fireplace, it produces heat and light. But when it is used improperly, fire threatens to consume everything in its path.

So it is with ambition. The Bible encourages us to learn to distinguish between godly ambition, which can produce great benefits, and selfish ambition, which can blaze out of control. Godly ambition yields a burning desire to know God and do what He asks. Selfish ambition produces the desire to bring credit and glory to yourself rather than to God. You can test your ambition by asking yourself this question: Is it leading you closer to God or farther away from Him?

Joyful are people of integrity, who follow the instructions of the LORD. Joyful are those who ... search for him with all their hearts.

PSALM 119:1-2

Make it your goal to live a quiet life, minding your own business and working with your hands, just as we instructed you before.

1 THESSALONIANS 4:11

My ambition has always been to preach the Good News where the name of Christ has never been heard.

ROMANS 15:20

WHY DO I GET ANGRY?

Anger is often a reaction to your pride being hurt. When you are confronted, rejected, ignored, or don't get your way, anger acts as a defense mechanism to protect your ego. It is common to feel angry when someone confronts you about your own sinful actions because you don't want others to know that you've done something wrong.

When anger begins to well up inside you, stop and ask yourself, *Who is really offended in this situation? Is this about God's honor or my pride? Am I acting out of humility or revenge?* Confession, forgiveness, and reconciliation will melt your anger away.

> The LORD accepted Abel and his gift, but he did not accept Cain and his gift. This made Cain very angry, and he looked dejected.
>
> GENESIS 4:4-5

> "Didn't I tell you?" the king of Israel exclaimed to Jehoshaphat. "He never prophesies anything but trouble for me. ... Put this man in prison, and feed him nothing but bread and water!"
>
> 1 KINGS 22:18, 27

> When Haman saw that Mordecai would not bow down or show him respect, he was filled with rage.
>
> ESTHER 3:5

A BALANCED LIFE

Living a balanced life means you honor God, others, and yourself with the way you use your gifts and spend your time and resources. It's easy to let your life get out of balance by overemphasizing one aspect of your responsibilities at the cost of others. God assures you that there is a time for everything, and there is time for everything He calls you to do.

Jesus, despite His power and the needs of those around Him, left much undone; yet He completed everything God had given Him to do. You will find true peace and contentment when you realize you don't have to do everything, just those things God created you to do. You will find balance when you know that in God's eyes you have done what you need to do.

For everything there is a season, a time for every activity under heaven.

ECCLESIASTES 3:1

I brought glory to you here on earth by completing the work you gave me to do. Now, Father, bring me into the glory we shared before the world began.

JOHN 17:4-5

All of you together are Christ's body, and each of you is a part of it.

1 CORINTHIANS 12:27

PREVENTING BURNOUT

Burnout is an overwhelming exhaustion and inability to push on, usually brought about by too much stress. We all experience times of burnout, when we feel tapped out emotionally, mentally, physically, and spiritually. In our fast-paced, 24-7 world, it isn't surprising that we become quickly exhausted.

Because burnout is so draining and paralyzing, you need to take care of your body and mind by eating right, exercising, and getting enough sleep and relaxation. One of the best ways to reduce burnout is to take time out to be close to God. When you draw close to Him, you can tap into His power, strength, peace, protection, and love. This will give you the strength to persevere through even the worst times of burnout.

I am exhausted and completely crushed. My groans come from an anguished heart.

PSALM 38:8

Only in returning to me and resting in me will you be saved. In quietness and confidence is your strength.

ISAIAH 30:15

Come to me, all of you who are weary and carry heavy burdens, and I will give you rest. ... You will find rest for your souls.

MATTHEW 11:28-29

TESTING BUILDS CHARACTER

It is a basic principle of life that adversity produces strength. Just as your muscles grow only when stretched to their limit, so your character grows only when the pressures of life push against it and test its strength. Developing strong character, therefore, is a process that takes time and constant attention. Your muscles will get flabby if you stop exercising.

Likewise, your character will get soft if you stop working on it. It may not be easy, but it is only through hard work that you will achieve great accomplishment and the sense of satisfaction that goes along with it. The pressure from pain, trials, and temptations will refine you so that over time you will be better equipped and more experienced to deal with them. Character building is hard work that always pays off, both now and for eternity.

Until the time came to fulfill his dreams, the LORD tested Joseph's character.

PSALM 105:19

Endurance develops strength of character, and character strengthens our confident hope of salvation.

ROMANS 5:4

The more you grow like this, the more productive and useful you will be in your knowledge of our Lord Jesus Christ.

2 PETER 1:8

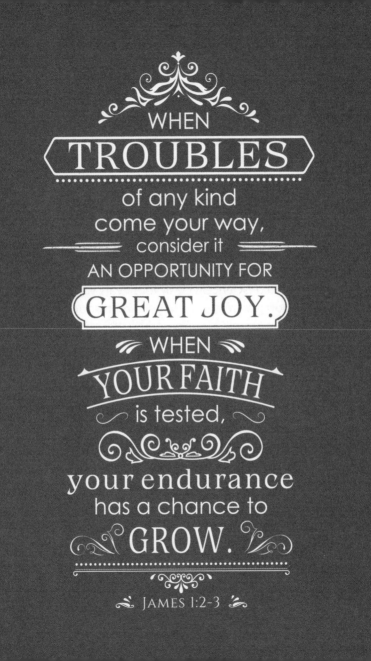

WHEN
TROUBLES
of any kind
come your way,
consider it
AN OPPORTUNITY FOR
GREAT JOY.
WHEN
YOUR FAITH
is tested,
your endurance
has a chance to
GROW.

JAMES 1:2-3

A CLEAR CONSCIENCE

When your motives are selfish or impure, it is only a matter of time before your actions become selfish and impure. God is far more concerned about the condition of your heart than He is with your external behavior. Your behavior always flows from what is in your heart, not the other way around.

Remember that God alone knows your heart. You may be able to fool others and even yourself, but you can't fool God. Welcome His examination. Then, like Paul, you can say that your conscience is clear. And when your conscience is clear, your heart will be open to God doing a great work in you and through you.

Learn to know the God of your ancestors intimately. Worship and serve him with your whole heart and a willing mind. For the LORD sees every heart and knows every plan and thought.

1 CHRONICLES 28:9

May the words of my mouth and the meditation of my heart be pleasing to you, O LORD, my rock and my redeemer.

PSALM 19:14

My conscience is clear, but that doesn't prove I'm right. It is the Lord himself who will examine me and decide.

1 CORINTHIANS 4:4

MAKING RIGHT DECISIONS

Making right decisions is like hiking; each step puts you a little further down the path. Sometimes making the right decision simply means being faithful in little things. God's will for you is to read His Word, obey Him, serve others, and do what is right.

If you make decisions to do His will today, you can be sure that you will be doing His will twenty years from now. Then when you approach the end of your life, you will be able to finish well and leave behind a legacy of faithfulness.

Commit your actions to the LORD, and your plans will succeed.

PROVERBS 16:3

Oh, that we might know the LORD! Let us press on to know him. He will respond to us as surely as the arrival of dawn or the coming of rains in early spring.

HOSEA 6:3

My steps have stayed on your path; I have not wavered from following you.

PSALM 17:5

Seek his will in all you do, and he will show you which path to take.

PROVERBS 3:6

HEALTHY DESIRES

God created desire within you as a means of expressing yourself. Desires are good and healthy when they are directed toward those things that are good and right and God-honoring. The same basic desire can be right or wrong, depending upon your motives and the object of your desire.

For example, the desire to love a woman is healthy and right when it is directed toward your wife. But that same desire directed toward anyone you are not married to is adultery.

The desire to lead an organization is healthy if your motive is to serve others, but it is unhealthy and wrong if your motive is to gain power or control over others. Your greatest desire must be for a relationship with God, which will influence all your other desires.

Hope deferred makes the heart sick, but a dream fulfilled is a tree of life.

PROVERBS 13:12

I desire you more than anything on earth.

PSALM 73:25

LORD, we show our trust in you by obeying your laws; our heart's desire is to glorify your name.

ISAIAH 26:8

If you look for me wholeheartedly, you will find me.

JEREMIAH 29:13

A GODLY EXAMPLE

The Bible teaches that parents bear the fundamental responsibility for spiritual education of children, and that spiritual values are most effectively taught when they are integrated into the fabric of daily family life. What would a child watching your life conclude about the importance of a relationship with God? As you strive to be a good example, remember God first thing in the morning, and fall asleep with Him on your mind. Remember God as the source of hope when you think you've lost all hope.

Remember God with a thankful heart when you have plenty, for you will need Him when you have little. Weave Him into the fabric of your life so your children and grandchildren will be trained from their earliest days to love God with grateful hearts.

You must commit yourselves wholeheartedly to these commands that I am giving you today. Repeat them again and again to your children. Talk about them when you are at home and when you are on the road, when you are going to bed and when you are getting up.

DEUTERONOMY 6:6-7

Take a new grip with your tired hands and strengthen your weak knees. Mark out a straight path for your feet so that those who are weak and lame will not fall but become strong.

HEBREWS 12:12-13

STRIVING FOR EXCELLENCE

God wants us to pursue excellence because doing so shows we care about doing things right, that we care about helping people to the best of our ability. Pursuing excellence helps others experience excellence by giving them a glimpse of God's character and inspiring them to pursue excellence themselves.

God initiated excellence in the beauty of His creation, and we are called to perpetuate it. Our lives display excellence when we consistently strive to model ourselves after Jesus Christ, who was perfect, and as we go about the work He has called us to do. We'll never be perfect in this life, but as we work toward that goal, we will model excellence to those around us.

God looked over all he had made, and he saw that it was very good!

GENESIS 1:31

Do you have the gift of helping others? Do it with all the strength and energy that God supplies.

1 PETER 4:11

Work willingly at whatever you do, as though you were working for the Lord rather than for people. Remember that the Lord will give you an inheritance as your reward, and that the Master you are serving is Christ.

COLOSSIANS 3:23-24

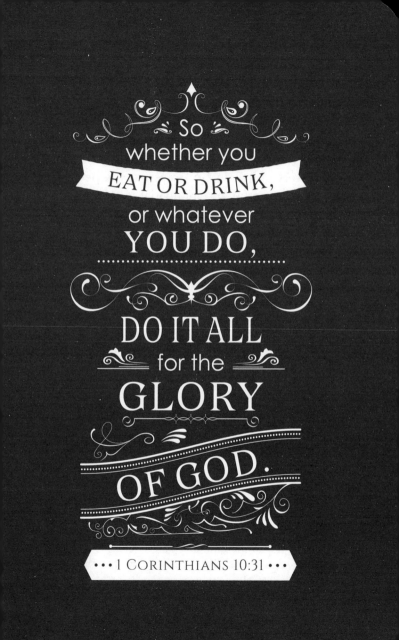

So whether you EAT OR DRINK, or whatever YOU DO, DO IT ALL for the GLORY OF GOD.

1 CORINTHIANS 10:31

GENTLENESS IS POWERFUL

You might wonder what gentleness can accomplish. Being gentle does not mean you should be anyone's doormat. God is the perfect example of gentleness, yet He is also a mighty warrior who defeats the powers of hell. In God's eyes, gentle people are the most powerful and influential in the world because they make an impact on others without the use of force or conflict.

Gentleness may be your most powerful weapon of influence because you can accomplish much more by gentleness than by coercion.

> The Holy Spirit produces this kind of fruit in our lives: love, joy, peace, patience, kindness, goodness, faithfulness, gentleness, and self-control.
>
> GALATIANS 5:22-23

> You should clothe yourselves instead with the beauty that comes from within, the unfading beauty of a gentle and quiet spirit, which is so precious to God.
>
> 1 PETER 3:4

> Pursue righteousness and a godly life, along with faith, love, perseverance, and gentleness.
>
> 1 TIMOTHY 6:11

> God blesses those who are humble, for they will inherit the whole earth.
>
> MATTHEW 5:5

A WORTHY GOAL

You harvest what you plant: Pumpkin seeds produce pumpkins, sunflower seeds produce sunflowers. That is why you should ask the Lord to plant within you a good heart so that your life will produce good thoughts, motives, and actions.

If any bad desires or thoughts remain, it is evidence that some bad seeds have also been planted, and you need to do some weeding. Complete renewal is not yet accomplished because none of us can be entirely pure in this life. But developing purity of mind and heart is one of the worthiest goals you can pursue. Is it one of your goals? More than anything else, a clean heart and mind will impact your relationship with God, your family, and your friends.

How might you be different a year from now—inside and outside—if you accomplished this goal?

Create in me a clean heart, O God. Renew a loyal spirit within me.

PSALM 51:10

Let the Spirit renew your thoughts and attitudes. Put on your new nature.

EPHESIANS 4:23-24

Let's not get tired of doing what is good. At just the right time we will reap a harvest of blessing if we don't give up.

GALATIANS 6:9

GUARDING YOUR HEART

Ultimately your actions come from your heart. What you do shows the condition of your heart. Left unchecked, wrong desires and thoughts will eventually result in wrong actions.

For example, if you allow yourself to think about having sex with someone who is not your spouse, your heart will begin to convince you that it's okay. The Bible says that "the human heart is the most deceitful of all things, and desperately wicked" (Jeremiah 17:9).

In other words, don't trust your emotions to tell you the difference between right and wrong. Trust God's Word; it comes from God's heart, which is good and perfect.

Guard your heart above all else, for it determines the course of your life.

PROVERBS 4:23

It is what comes from inside that defiles you. For from within, out of a person's heart, come evil thoughts, sexual immorality, … lustful desires.

MARK 7:20-22

Your eye is a lamp that provides light for your body. When your eye is good, your whole body is filled with light.

LUKE 11:34

LIVING A HOLY LIFE

Think of holiness as both a journey and a final destination. To be completely holy is to be sinless, pure, and perfect before God. Of course, no one is perfect, but that is our ultimate goal. We will reach that final destination when we stand before God in heaven. But holiness also means to be different, to be set apart by God for a specific purpose.

We are to be different from the rest of the world. Our lives are to be a journey toward holiness so that we become a little more pure and sinless with each passing day. If you strive to be holy on your earthly journey, you will one day arrive at your final destination and stand holy before God.

I am writing ... to you who have been called by God to be his own holy people. He made you holy by means of Christ Jesus, just as he did for all people everywhere who call on the name of our Lord Jesus Christ, their Lord and ours.

1 CORINTHIANS 1:2

You were cleansed; you were made holy.

1 CORINTHIANS 6:11

I plead with you to give your bodies to God because of all he has done for you. Let them be a living and holy sacrifice—the kind he will find acceptable.

ROMANS 12:1

THE POWER OF THE SPIRIT

The Holy Spirit is the power of God, and He lives in every believer. When you give control of your life to the Lord, the Holy Spirit releases His power within you—power to resist temptation, to serve and love God and others, to endure when you are at the end of your rope, to have wisdom in all circumstances, and to persevere in living for God here on earth with the promise of eternal life in heaven.

Through His Spirit, God gives you the energy and the resources you need to do whatever He asks you to do.

> I pray that from his glorious, unlimited resources he will empower you with inner strength through his Spirit.
>
> EPHESIANS 3:16

> You will receive power when the Holy Spirit comes upon you. And you will be my witnesses, telling people about me everywhere.
>
> ACTS 1:8

> We have received God's Spirit (not the world's spirit), so we can know the wonderful things God has freely given us.
>
> 1 CORINTHIANS 2:12

> Let the Holy Spirit guide your lives. Then you won't be doing what your sinful nature craves.
>
> GALATIANS 5:16

For

THE LORD

is the

SPIRIT

&

wherever the

SPIRIT

of the Lord is,

there is

FREEDOM.

2 CORINTHIANS 3:17

LASTING JOY

There is a difference between joy and happiness. Happiness, which is temporary, is a reaction to events in your life. Joy, which is strong and lasting, happens in spite of your circumstances.

This kind of joy can only happen by following God and living according to His principles. God does not promise constant happiness; in fact, the Bible assures us that we will have problems because we live in a fallen world. But God does promise lasting joy to those who follow Him.

This kind of joy stays with you despite your problems because you know that God is with you, that He will help you through them, and that one day He will take them all away. You can have this lasting joy even when you don't feel happy.

They are being tested by many troubles, and they are very poor. But they are also filled with abundant joy, which has overflowed in rich generosity.

2 CORINTHIANS 8:2

When troubles come your way, consider it an opportunity for great joy.

JAMES 1:2

Now all glory to God, who is able to keep you from falling away and will bring you with great joy into his glorious presence without a single fault.

JUDE 1:24

A LOVE FOR GOD

Love is often defined in romantic or sentimental terms. Love is indeed a feeling, but it is also more than that. It is a commitment that both protects and produces passionate feelings. Because it is a commitment, love is not dependent on warm feelings alone but on a consistent and courageous decision to extend yourself for the well-being of someone else.

Loving feelings can produce commitment, but commitment can also produce loving feelings. Jesus perfectly demonstrated God's unconditional love for you when He made the loving commitment to lay down His life to save you from your sins. When you love God with all your heart, soul, and strength, you are making a commitment to develop a relationship with the Creator of the universe, who loved you first and daily pursues you with His love.

You must love the LORD your God with all your heart, all your soul, and all your strength.

DEUTERONOMY 6:5

I love the LORD because he hears my voice and my prayer for mercy.

PSALM 116:1

When you obey my commandments, you remain in my love. ... I have told you these things so that you will be filled with my joy. Yes, your joy will overflow!

JOHN 15:10-11

A STRONG MARRIAGE

Being united in serving the Lord is one key to a strong marriage. Sexual faithfulness to your wife is another key to a strong and happy marriage. Without faithfulness, there will be no trust or intimacy. Commitment to stay together no matter what is essential for a strong and lasting marriage.

Self-sacrifice is essential to a strong marriage; thinking of your wife's needs and interests ahead of your own. Praying with each other and for each other helps to strengthen your marriage. Mutual submission in serving one another is one key to a strong marriage. Unconditional love is essential for a strong marriage. Consistently demonstrating unconditional love is perhaps the hardest thing to do in marriage, but it is the most important key to having a great relationship and winning over the heart of your wife.

Rejoice in the wife of your youth. ... Let her breasts satisfy you always. May you always be captivated by her love.

PROVERBS 5:18-19

Since they are no longer two but one, let no one split apart what God has joined together.

MATTHEW 19:6

"A man leaves his father and mother and is joined to his wife, and the two are united into one."

EPHESIANS 5:31

OVERCOMING THE PAST

How you view your past affects how you live in the present and in the future. Some of us have a past containing a strong spiritual heritage from loving parents and mentors. Don't take that for granted; use it to help and minister to others.

Some of us have a past filled with regret over actions that were wrong or hurtful. Some of us have a tragic past marred by abuse, neglect, violence, or the shameful acts of other people. No matter what you've done or what's been done to you, God is ready to forgive you, heal you, cleanse you of sin and guilt, and give you a new start—fully forgiven. God wants to give you a new present and future—and He can if you'll let Him. God can remove your regret, guilt, and shame, and you can be free to live in peace with purpose and joy.

I will never forget your commandments, for by them you give me life.

PSALM 119: 93

Though your sins are like scarlet, I will make them as white as snow. Though they are red like crimson, I will make them as white as wool.

ISAIAH 1:18

I will forgive their wickedness, and I will never again remember their sins.

HEBREWS 8:12

PEACE IN THE MIDST OF CHANGE

Change is one thing that never changes. You can be sure that you will always face new challenges. Don't be upset when your plans are thwarted. Instead, build your life on the changeless principles and promises that God gives you in His Word.

When you experience upheaval, turn to God's Word to maintain your perspective and stay grounded. Remember the inheritance that awaits you in heaven, beyond change and decay, and you will have peace. It is essential that you approach life with this eternal perspective. It gives you the security of knowing that your future is in God's hands. As an added bonus, you are assured that God's power, comfort, and peace are available to you now.

[Lord,] you are always the same.

HEBREWS 1:12

Heaven and earth will disappear, but my words will never disappear.

MARK 13:31

I am leaving you with a gift—peace of mind and heart. And the peace I give is a gift the world cannot give. So don't be troubled or afraid.

JOHN 14:27

You will keep in perfect peace all who trust in you, all whose thoughts are fixed on you!

ISAIAH 26:3

In PEACE

I will lie down
and sleep,
for
YOU ALONE,

O LORD,

will keep me
SAFE.

PSALM 4:8

PERSEVERE THROUGH TOUGH TIMES

Perseverance can be defined as "courage stretched out." Although God sometimes delivers His people from difficult or painful circumstances, He often calls us to courageous and enduring faithfulness in the midst of trials. According to the Bible, perseverance is not just enduring difficult situations; it is overcoming them with obedience, hope, and joy.

If you don't learn to persevere through your struggles, you will fall into the habit of giving up. But when you persevere until you come out on the other side, you grow stronger in your faith. You see the benefits of obeying God, and you develop the confidence that when problems come again, you will get through them with God's help.

We were crushed and overwhelmed beyond our ability to endure, and we thought we would never live through it. In fact, we expected to die. But as a result, we stopped relying on ourselves and learned to rely only on God.

2 CORINTHIANS 1:8-9

When troubles come your way, consider it an opportunity for great joy. For you know that when your faith is tested, your endurance has a chance to grow.

JAMES 1:2-3

GOD'S PLANS FOR YOU

Joseph's willingness to use his God-given gifts to help the Egyptians plan for seven years of famine allowed God's plan to be carried out. It's fine to ask God to bless your plans, but you should also be willing to use your gifts and abilities to help carry out God's plans. What a wonderful moment it is when God uses you to implement His plan!

How do you know what work God wants you to be a part of? The first step is to have an open mind and an obedient heart, like Joseph did. The path of obedience will always take you in the right direction. As you follow God, plan to become a part of His plan.

Joseph's suggestions were well received by Pharaoh and his officials. So Pharaoh asked his officials, "Can we find anyone else like this man so obviously filled with the spirit of God?"

GENESIS 41:37-38

What you ought to say is, "If the Lord wants us to, we will live and do this or that."

JAMES 4:15

Trust in the LORD with all your heart; do not depend on your own understanding. Seek his will in all you do, and he will show you which path to take.

PROVERBS 3:5-6

THE POWER OF GOD

Imagine experiencing the earth's strongest earth-quake, tallest tsunami, wildest volcano, and most devastating hurricane—all at the same time. This cannot even begin to compare to God's power! He is the creator of all these phenomena, and what is created is never more powerful than the creator.

This same God has the power to calm the storms in your heart, to dry up a flood of fear, to quench the lust for sin, and to control the whirlwind of your life. You must put more trust in God's power than your own. Thankfully, God's power does not depend on human strength. The same power God used to create the world and defeat Satan will be available to you.

I also pray that you will understand the incredible greatness of God's power for us who believe him. This is the same mighty power that raised Christ from the dead and seated him in the place of honor at God's right hand in the heavenly realms.

EPHESIANS 1:19-20

I work and struggle so hard, depending on Christ's mighty power that works within me.

COLOSSIANS 1:29

All glory to God, who is able, through his mighty power at work within us, to accomplish infinitely more than we might ask or think.

EPHESIANS 3:20

GOD ALWAYS LISTENS

God listens carefully to every prayer and answers each one. His answer may be yes, no, or wait, just as loving parents might give each of these three responses to the requests of their child. Answering yes to every request would spoil you and endanger your well-being. Answering no to every request would be vindictive, stingy, and hard on your spirit. Answering wait to every request would frustrate you.

God always answers your prayers according to what He knows is best for you. Knowing that God always listens and answers should inspire you to pray continually, even if His answer is not always the one you wanted.

I love the LORD because he hears my voice and my prayer for mercy.

PSALM 116:1

Three different times I begged the Lord to take it away. Each time he said, "My grace is all you need. My power works best in weakness."

2 CORINTHIANS 12:8-9

If you remain in me and my words remain in you, you may ask for anything you want, and it will be granted!

JOHN 15:7

A PRAYERFUL ATTITUDE

The Bible teaches that God honors and acknowledges the prayers of the humble. Humility comes when you recognize that you need God.

Before you ask with boldness, fall to your knees in humility. When you humbly come to God, it shows that you recognize His sovereignty. Then your prayers will be better aligned with His plans for you. Following God's will for your life will lead you toward what is good and right and away from sin and harm.

> O my people, trust in him at all times. Pour out your heart to him, for God is our refuge.
>
> PSALM 62:8

> Devote yourselves to prayer with an alert mind and a thankful heart.
>
> COLOSSIANS 4:2

> [Jesus prayed,] "Father, if you are willing, please take this cup of suffering away from me. Yet I want your will to be done, not mine."
>
> LUKE 22:42

> Humble yourselves under the mighty power of God, and at the right time he will lift you up in honor.
>
> 1 PETER 5:6

REJOICE in our CONFIDENT HOPE. BE PATIENT in trouble & keep on PRAYING.

ROMANS 12:12

GENUINE FAITH

In our world we seem to find it increasingly easy to say, "I don't want to get involved." When we see someone in need or notice something we could do to help others, we may be tempted to turn a blind eye and pretend we don't notice. We may hope someone else will do something about it.

God reminds us that pretending to care about the needy, or pretending not to notice when someone needs help, or pretending there's nothing you can do, are all forms of hypocrisy. Genuine faith is compassionate and active, ready and willing to go the extra mile to help those in need.

Live wisely among those who are not believers, and make the most of every opportunity. Let your conversation be gracious and attractive so that you will have the right response for everyone.

COLOSSIANS 4:5-6

Don't just pretend to love others. Really love them. Hate what is wrong. Hold tightly to what is good.

ROMANS 12:9

Dear children, let's not merely say that we love each other; let us show the truth by our actions. Our actions will show that we belong to the truth, so we will be confident when we stand before God.

1 JOHN 3:18-19

SETTING PRIORITIES

What are the things that matter most in life, that are true priorities? How can we distinguish true priorities from lesser ones? The answer is this: Don't confuse what's urgent with what's important. You must set your priorities first.

Don't let everyone else decide what your day should look like—that should be between you and God. If you make God your first priority, He will give you the proper perspective on the rest of the activities in your day. Ask God to show you what is worth being concerned about.

Seek his will in all you do, and he will show you which path to take.

PROVERBS 3:6

Wherever your treasure is, there the desires of your heart will also be.

LUKE 12:34

As I looked at everything I had worked so hard to accomplish, it was all so meaningless—like chasing the wind. There was nothing really worthwhile anywhere.

ECCLESIASTES 2:11

Seek the Kingdom of God above all else, and live righteously, and he will give you everything you need.

MATTHEW 6:33

GOD'S PROVISION

There's a big difference between wants and needs, though we often have trouble making that distinction. When you understand what you truly need and then see how God provides it, you will realize how much God cares for you.

God doesn't promise to give you a lot of possessions, but He does promise to help you possess the qualities that reflect His nature so you can accomplish His plan for you. He doesn't promise to preserve your physical life, but He does promise to take care of your soul for all eternity if you believe in Him and are committed to Him.

God will generously provide all you need. Then you will always have everything you need and plenty left over to share with others. As the Scriptures say, "They share freely and give generously to the poor. Their good deeds will be remembered forever."

2 CORINTHIANS 9:8-9

This same God who takes care of me will supply all your needs from his glorious riches, which have been given to us in Christ Jesus.

PHILIPPIANS 4:19

I will be your God throughout your lifetime—until your hair is white with age. I made you, and I will care for you. I will carry you along and save you.

ISAIAH 46:4

WHAT IS MY PURPOSE?

According to the Bible, your purpose is to be inspired with a vision of how God can best use you to accomplish His goals. God has both a general purpose and a specific purpose for you. In a general sense, you have been chosen by God to let the love of Jesus shine through you to make an impact on others.

More specifically, God has given you unique spiritual gifts and wants you to use them to make a contribution within your sphere of influence. The more you fulfill your general purpose, the clearer your specific purpose will become.

Your ultimate goal in life should not be to reach the destinations you want but to reach the destinations God wants for you. As you passionately pursue the purpose God has assigned you, God promises to give your life greater meaning, lasting significance, and eternal results.

I cry out to God Most High, to God who will fulfill his purpose for me.

PSALM 57:2

My life is worth nothing to me unless I use it for finishing the work assigned me by the Lord Jesus— the work of telling others the Good News.

ACTS 20:24

You didn't choose me. I chose you. I appointed you to go and produce lasting fruit.

JOHN 15:16

DON'T QUIT

When God has called you to a task, you shouldn't give up. Not only will you miss out on the great blessing of reaching your goal, you might also experience God's discipline for not trusting Him to help you get there.

Just because God asks you to do something doesn't mean it will be easy. In fact, the more important the task, the harder it often is. If you know that God is in what you are doing or is taking you a certain direction, don't give up just because the going gets tough. If anything, that should tell you that you are headed in the right direction. Keep moving forward boldly in faith.

Be strong and courageous, and do the work. Don't be afraid or discouraged, for the LORD God, my God, is with you. He will not fail you or forsake you. He will see to it that all the work … is finished correctly.

1 CHRONICLES 28:20

We are pressed on every side by troubles, but we are not crushed. We know that God, who raised the Lord Jesus, will also raise us with Jesus and present us to himself together with you. That is why we never give up.

2 CORINTHIANS 4:8, 14-16

Let's not get tired of doing what is good. At just the right time we will reap a harvest of blessing if we don't give up.

GALATIANS 6:9

I have
fought the

GOOD FIGHT,

I have

finished
THE RACE
&

I have remained

FAITHFUL.

2 TIMOTHY 4:7

DEALING WITH REGRETS

When you come to faith in Jesus, He forgives your sins—all of them. He actually forgets your past, and He gives you a fresh start. You still have to live with the consequences of your actions because those cannot be retracted. But because God forgives and forgets, you can move forward without the heavy burden of regret. Because God no longer holds your past against you, you no longer need to hold it against yourself. You can be free from self-condemnation.

Don't let regret paralyze you; let God's forgiveness motivate you toward positive action for Him in the future. It is a divine moment when you truly grasp the power of God's healing forgiveness and are able to turn your regrets into resolve.

This means that anyone who belongs to Christ has become a new person. The old life is gone; a new life has begun!

2 CORINTHIANS 5:17

David also spoke of this when he described the happiness of those who are declared righteous without working for it: "Oh, what joy for those whose disobedience is forgiven, whose sins are put out of sight. Yes, what joy for those whose record the Lord has cleared of sin."

ROMANS 4:6-8

FEMALE FRIENDS

Friendships with women are an important part of most men's lives, but they can also be a powerful source of temptation. Jesus had many female friends, some of whom supported His ministry and even traveled with Him, so it is appropriate for men to have healthy friendships with women.

However, married men must be extra cautious to ensure that any friendships with other women do not turn into emotional relationships in which strong feelings can become inappropriate intimacy.

This betrays the trust and commitment a man shares with his wife. Here are three ways to safeguard yourself: Never be alone with a female friend; avoid talking about your marital problems; always treat other women with great respect.

Treat older women as you would your mother, and treat younger women with all purity as you would your own sisters.

1 TIMOTHY 5:2

Anyone who even looks at a woman with lust has already committed adultery with her in his heart.

MATTHEW 5:28

God blesses those whose hearts are pure, for they will see God.

MATTHEW 5:8

STARTING OVER

Renewal begins with God's compassion and a heart that is ready for change. When the two are brought together, renewal will happen. God will restore any heart that seeks a new start. That new start begins when you turn to God and turn away from what has been bringing you down. Ask God to forgive your sin, which is working inside you to poison everything you do.

Thank God that His forgiveness is not based on the magnitude of our sin but on the magnitude of His love. No sin is too great for God's complete and unconditional love. A heart that truly wants to change is a heart that is ready for the renewal that only God's Spirit can bring.

I will give you a new heart, and I will put a new spirit in you. I will take out your stony, stubborn heart and give you a tender, responsive heart.

EZEKIEL 36:26

"Come now, let's settle this," says the LORD. "Though your sins are like scarlet, I will make them as white as snow. Though they are red like crimson, I will make them as white as wool."

ISAIAH 1:18

Create in me a clean heart, O God. Renew a loyal spirit within me.

PSALM 51:10

THE RIGHT DIRECTION

Have you ever had the experience of driving in an unfamiliar city and suddenly realizing that you were going the wrong way on a one-way street? What you do next is very much like the biblical idea of repentance—you make a U-turn and change your direction as fast as you can.

Repentance is motivated by the realization that you have taken the wrong way in life. Repentance is admitting your sin and making a commitment, with God's help, to change the direction of your life. Repentance is essential because it is the only way to arrive at your desired destination—heaven.

Repentance makes change possible so you can experience God's fullest blessings, both now and for eternity. Are you going in the right direction?

There is forgiveness of sins for all who repent.

LUKE 24:47

Repent of your sins and turn to God, so that your sins may be wiped away.

ACTS 3:19

If my people who are called by my name will humble themselves and pray and seek my face and turn from their wicked ways, I will hear from heaven and will forgive their sins and restore their land.

2 CHRONICLES 7:14

A GOOD REPUTATION

People often think that your personal life does not matter as long as you perform well on the job or look good in public. God, however, does not make a distinction between your public life and your private life. Justice, righteousness, integrity, mercy, honesty, fairness, and faithfulness are essential traits of a godly person's character and reputation because they reflect God's character.

You will develop a good reputation when you display the same godly integrity in private as you do in public. What matters most is not what others think of you but what God thinks of you. This perspective helps you maintain consistency between your public life and private life.

Work willingly at whatever you do, as though you were working for the Lord rather than for people.

COLOSSIANS 3:23

Choose a good reputation over great riches; being held in high esteem is better than silver or gold.

PROVERBS 22:1

Never let loyalty and kindness leave you! Tie them around your neck as a reminder. Write them deep within your heart. Then you will find favor with both God and people, and you will earn a good reputation.

PROVERBS 3:3-4

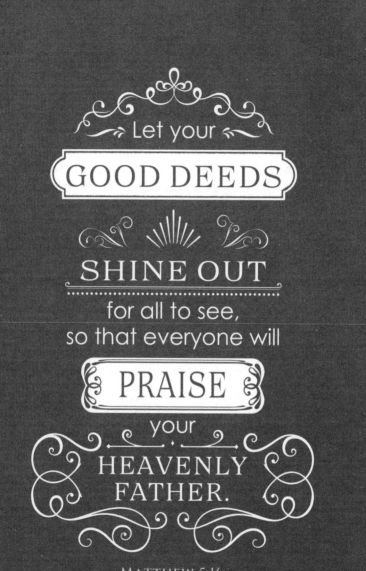

Let your

GOOD DEEDS

SHINE OUT

for all to see,
so that everyone will

PRAISE

your

HEAVENLY
FATHER.

MATTHEW 5:16

SHOWING RESPECT

Every person has the need to feel respected. When David gave the order for Joab's plan to be put into effect, Joab was overjoyed at the sense of his own worth.

You can show respect to others in several ways: (1) Listen. Good listening gives dignity to others by putting them at the center of your attention. (2) Affirm. Saying "You're right" or "That's a good idea" is very powerful. (3) Act. Following through on other people's suggestions is the strongest possible statement of your respect for them. When it is necessary to disagree with others, you should do so with a respectful attitude.

Dear brothers and sisters, honor those who are your leaders in the Lord's work. ... Show them great respect and wholehearted love because of their work.

1 THESSALONIANS 5:12-13

A despised Samaritan came along, and when he saw the man, he felt compassion for him. Going over to him, the Samaritan soothed his wounds.

LUKE 10:33-34

Joab bowed with his face to the ground in deep respect and said, "At last I know that I have gained your approval, my lord the king, for you have granted me this request!"

2 SAMUEL 14:22

TAKE TIME TO REST

From God's own example in Genesis to the promises He makes in the New Testament, it is clear that God wants us to have rest and refreshment for our body and soul. Why would the omnipotent God of the universe rest after doing the work of creation? Surely it wasn't because the Almighty was tired! The answer is that God, in ceasing from His work, proclaimed His rest to be holy. God knew that we would need to cease from our work to care for our physical and spiritual needs.

Work is good, but it must be balanced with regular rest and attention to the health of your soul. Otherwise, you might miss the divine opportunities God sends your way. Make sure to carve out regular times for worship and spiritual refreshment.

It is a permanent sign of my covenant with the people of Israel. For in six days the LORD made heaven and earth, but on the seventh day he stopped working and was refreshed.

EXODUS 31:17

It is useless for you to work so hard from early morning until late at night, anxiously working for food to eat; for God gives rest to his loved ones.

PSALM 127:2

Come to me, all of you who are weary and carry heavy burdens, and I will give you rest.

MATTHEW 11:28

TAKING RISKS

The Bible tells us that the Christian life is risky; spiritual growth and success can only occur with some level of risk. Taking foolish chances is not the same as taking a risk—it's either stupidity, or it's being totally unrealistic about your goals.

Taking a risk entails having a worthy goal, a good chance of achieving it, and a strong dose of confidence. Risk-taking is necessary if you want to grow in your relationship with God. When He calls you to do something that is out of your comfort zone, obey Him despite the risk of failing, and trust Him to help you succeed.

Though it may seem like a moment of risk, it will actually be an incredible moment of growth.

A prudent person foresees danger and takes precautions. The simpleton goes blindly on and suffers the consequences.

PROVERBS 22:3

Do not be afraid of the terrors of the night, nor the arrow that flies in the day.

PSALM 91:5

Commit everything you do to the LORD. Trust him, and he will help you.

PSALM 37:5

THE LANGUAGE OF LOVE

God created the concept of intimate love between husband and wife. He also created an even deeper kind of love—the love between Creator and the created. God romances you in a way; He longs to have a deeper relationship with you, to be your God, to captivate you, to give you joy and peace. He wants your relationship with Him to continue happily ever after, for all eternity.

Romantic love between a husband and a wife is a picture of this deeper love that God desires to share with each person He has created. As you learn to romance your wife, you will see more clearly the way God romances all His people, wooing them into a lifelong, loyal, beautiful relationship with Him.

Like a lily among thistles is my darling among young women …

SONG OF SONGS 2:2

Drink water from your own well—share your love only with your wife. Why spill the water of your springs in the streets, having sex with just anyone? You should reserve it for yourselves. Never share it with strangers.

PROVERBS 5:15-17

"I have loved you, my people, with an everlasting love. With unfailing love I have drawn you to myself."

JEREMIAH 31:3

THE SACRIFICE FOR SIN

Today we are desensitized to the seriousness of sin, but it is just as serious to God as it has always been. Sin separates us from God. God is holy; we are not. Holiness and sin cannot coexist.

In Old Testament days, God provided a way for the sins of His people to be removed so they could be holy in His eyes. When Jesus died on the cross, He transferred the sins of all people for all time onto Himself. No more sacrifices need to be made. Jesus was the final sacrifice.

All you must do is recognize and confess your sin before God, then accept His gift of forgiveness. Whenever you make a sacrifice by giving something up for someone else, you can be reminded in some small way of God's sacrifice.

This is real love—not that we loved God, but that he loved us and sent his Son as a sacrifice to take away our sins.

1 JOHN 4:10

He personally carried our sins in his body on the cross so that we can be dead to sin and live for what is right. By his wounds you are healed.

1 PETER 2:24

Without the shedding of blood, there is no forgiveness.

HEBREWS 9:22

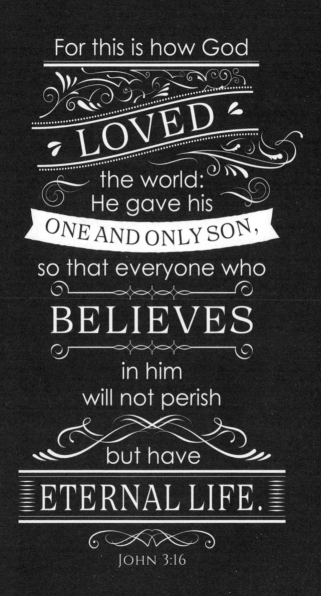

For this is how God

LOVED

the world:
He gave his
ONE AND ONLY SON,

so that everyone who

BELIEVES

in him
will not perish

but have

ETERNAL LIFE.

JOHN 3:16

STRIVING FOR SELF-CONTROL

Self-control is one of the hardest character traits to maintain because it means denying what comes naturally to your sinful nature and replacing it with a godly response.

Developing self-control is a lifelong endeavor because just when you think you have one area of your life mastered, another area gets out of control. Sometimes it seems almost impossible to control your thoughts, your words, and your physical appetites. But self-control saves you from the consequences of giving in to sin and bad habits.

Self-control begins with God's work in you, but it requires your effort as well. Just as a gifted musician or athlete must develop skills, strength, and coordination through intentional effort, striving for spiritual accomplishments must be intentional as well.

Train yourself to be godly. Physical training is good, but training for godliness is much better.

1 TIMOTHY 4:7-8

Better to have self-control than to conquer a city.

PROVERBS 16:32

Supplement your faith with a generous provision of moral excellence, and moral excellence with knowledge, and knowledge with self-control, and self-control with patient endurance, and patient endurance with godliness.

2 PETER 1:5-6

A HEALTHY SELF-ESTEEM

Your sufficiency is in God. Your value is tied to the value He places on you and the purpose for which He created you. That makes you a man of great value indeed. If you struggle with insecurities, perhaps you are measuring your value by the wrong standards.

The only thing that matters—and the only way to become confident—is to find your value as a creation and a masterpiece of God. When you understand how much God loves you, you will feel more confident in yourself. You should have a healthy self-esteem because with God you are capable of doing far more than you ever could have dreamed.

We are God's masterpiece. He has created us anew in Christ Jesus, so we can do the good things he planned for us long ago.

EPHESIANS 2:10

Not a single sparrow can fall to the ground without your Father knowing it. … You are more valuable to God than a whole flock of sparrows.

MATTHEW 10:29-31

Be honest in your evaluation of yourselves, measuring yourselves by the faith God has given us.

ROMANS 12:3

How precious are your thoughts about me, O God.

PSALM 139:17

SERVING OTHERS

Jesus teaches that the highest goal in life is to be a servant. He places such a high value on serving because it is centered on others rather than yourself, and serving others is the essence of effective Christian living.

When you are connected to Jesus, He turns your simple acts of service into something profound and purposeful. For example, He turns your simple act of singing into a profound chorus of praise that ministers to an entire congregation. He turns your simple act of tithing into a profound act of mercy that touches the heart of the needy person who benefits from it.

When you step out in faith to serve others, God turns your simple acts into profound works for His Kingdom.

You have been called to live in freedom, my brothers and sisters. But don't use your freedom to satisfy your sinful nature. Instead, use your freedom to serve one another in love.

GALATIANS 5:13

Whoever wants to be a leader among you must be your servant. ... For even the Son of Man came not to be served but to serve others and to give his life as a ransom for many.

MATTHEW 20:26-28

USE YOUR SPIRITUAL GIFTS

God gives each individual, including you, a spiritual gift and a special ministry in the church where you can use your gifts to help and encourage others and bring glory to His name.

When you use your spiritual gifts, you help fulfill the purpose for which God made you. You can never use up these spiritual gifts; rather, the more you use them, the more they grow, allowing you to make a greater contribution within your sphere of influence. Using your spiritual gifts will give you plenty of opportunities when you find your greatest area of effectiveness for God and do your best work for Him by helping others.

A spiritual gift is given to each of us so we can help each other. To one person the Spirit gives the ability to give wise advice; to another the same Spirit gives a message of special knowledge. The same Spirit gives great faith to another, and to someone else the one Spirit gives the gift of healing. ... In fact, some parts of the body that seem weakest and least important are actually the most necessary.

1 CORINTHIANS 12:7-11, 22

God has given each of you a gift from his great variety of spiritual gifts. Use them well to serve one another.

1 PETER 4:10

IN GOD'S STRENGTH

How do you get spiritual strength? First, recognize that the power God used to raise Jesus from the dead is the same power that will raise you from the dead if you believe in Him. And that same power is available to you now so you can live more effectively and courageously for Him.

Next, realize that God promises to give you inner strength through the power of His own Holy Spirit when you depend on Him and trust Him to do what is best for you.

Finally, remember that God's power works best through your weaknesses. When you are weak and limited, God will supply the strength to help you overcome great obstacles. God loves to work through your weaknesses because then everyone can see that it is Him, not you, supplying the strength.

I pray that from his glorious, unlimited resources he will empower you with inner strength through his Spirit. ... Now all glory to God, who is able, through his mighty power at work within us, to accomplish infinitely more than we might ask or think.

EPHESIANS 3:16, 20

Physical training is good, but training for godliness is much better, promising benefits in this life and in the life to come.

1 TIMOTHY 4:8

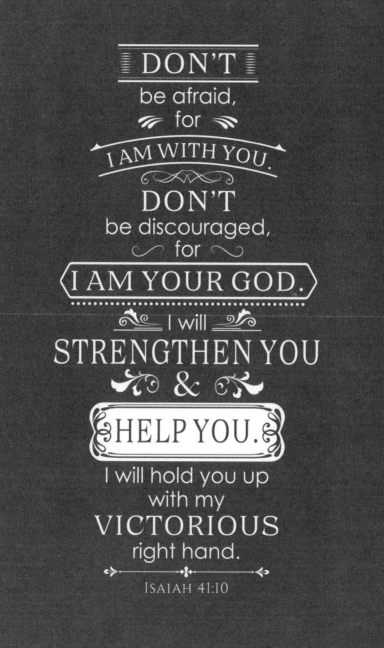

DON'T be afraid, for **I AM WITH YOU.** **DON'T** be discouraged, for **I AM YOUR GOD.** I will **STRENGTHEN YOU** & **HELP YOU.** I will hold you up with my **VICTORIOUS** right hand.

ISAIAH 41:10

TRUE SUCCESS

According to God's standards, success is measured not by material assets but by spiritual assets; not by what you have but by who you are; not by what you know but by who you know.

Some people are successful both by the world's standards and by God's standards. There is nothing wrong with that, but it is also rare. We get into trouble when we gain material or worldly success at the expense of true success as God defines it. How well you have succeeded in what God considers important counts in every way. Partnering with God in this life is the best way to ensure success in the next.

Our goal is to please him. For we must all stand before Christ to be judged. We will each receive whatever we deserve for the good or evil we have done in this earthly body.

2 CORINTHIANS 5:9-10

Commit your actions to the LORD, and your plans will succeed.

PROVERBS 16:3

Study this Book of Instruction continually. Meditate on it day and night so you will be sure to obey everything written in it. Only then will you prosper and succeed in all you do.

JOSHUA 1:8-9

WHEN TO SURRENDER

In the spiritual realm we fight two great battles, and surrender plays a part in both. On the one hand, we fight against sin and its control in our lives. If we are not allied with God, we will surrender to sin and its deadly consequences.

On the other hand, we often foolishly fight against God and His will for us because we want to have ultimate control over our lives. This is the battle in which surrender is necessary and positive. You surrender to God when you finally realize that you are powerless to defeat sin by yourself, and you give control of your life to God. It is only when you have God on your side that you can be victorious in your battle to defeat sin and pursue a better life now and in eternity.

> [Jesus] said, "If any of you wants to be my follower, you must turn from your selfish ways, take up your cross, and follow me."
>
> MARK 8:34

> You cannot become my disciple without giving up everything you own.
>
> LUKE 14:33

> Those who are dominated by the sinful nature think about sinful things, but those who are controlled by the Holy Spirit think about things that please the Spirit.
>
> ROMANS 8:5

FLEEING TEMPTATION

While Samson was in town, he noticed a beautiful woman. Temptation often begins with the eyes and travels quickly to the heart. What you do immediately after you see something or someone that poses a temptation for you will affect your thoughts and actions beyond the situation at hand.

If you let your eyes linger where they shouldn't, your mind will follow and will find ways to justify your gaze. Then your heart will start tugging you in that direction. The first step in avoiding temptation is taking your eyes off whatever may be tempting you.

You have heard the commandment that says, "You must not commit adultery." But I say, anyone who even looks at a woman with lust has already committed adultery with her in his heart.

MATTHEW 5:27-28

So guard your heart; do not be unfaithful to your wife.

MALACHI 2:16

The temptations in your life are no different from what others experience. And God is faithful. He will not allow the temptation to be more than you can stand. When you are tempted, he will show you a way out so that you can endure.

1 CORINTHIANS 10:13

TIMES OF TESTING

Our character and spiritual commitment are tested by the fires of hardship, persecution, and suffering. The Bible distinguishes between *temptation*, which Satan uses to lead us into sin, and *testing*, which God uses to purify us and move us toward spiritual growth and maturity. Out of testing comes a more committed faith.

Just as commercial products are tested so that their performance can be strengthened, so also God tests your faith to strengthen you so you can accomplish all God wants you to do. When you feel like your faith is being tested, see it as God working in your life to get your attention and to strengthen your relationship with Him.

The LORD your God is testing you to see if you truly love him with all your heart and soul.

DEUTERONOMY 13:3

God blesses those who patiently endure testing and temptation. Afterward they will receive the crown of life that God has promised to those who love him. And remember, when you are being tempted, do not say, "God is tempting me." God is never tempted to do wrong, and he never tempts anyone else.

JAMES 1:12-13

THANKFUL IN ALL CIRCUMSTANCES

The difficulties of life come for many reasons. You may be experiencing the consequences of your own sin; you may be suffering because of someone else's sin; you may be caught in unfortunate circumstances that are really no one's fault. God may be testing your faith, or Satan may be targeting you to disrupt your godly influence on others and to discourage your faith.

In any of these difficult circumstances, there are still reasons to thank God. He redeems your mistakes, teaches you wisdom through adversity, promises to help you through tough times, and guarantees you eternal life that is free from suffering. A God who redeems all troubles is a God worthy of praise and thanksgiving.

Joseph replied, "Don't be afraid of me. Am I God, that I can punish you? You intended to harm me, but God intended it all for good."

GENESIS 50:19-20

Be thankful in all circumstances, for this is God's will for you who belong to Christ Jesus.

1 THESSALONIANS 5:18

He will wipe every tear from their eyes, and there will be no more death or sorrow or crying or pain. All these things are gone forever.

REVELATION 21:4

Let all that I am

PRAISE

the LORD;

with my

WHOLE HEART,

I will praise his

HOLY NAME.

PSALM 103:1

PURE THOUGHTS

Controlling our thought life is perhaps one of the greatest struggles men face. Even if you do not immediately act on your thoughts, they do shape your attitudes and eventually your actions.

You must allow God to change the way you think by focusing your thoughts on Him and on anything that is true, honorable, right, pure, lovely, admirable, excellent, and worthy of praise. You can begin by reading Scripture, meditating on it, and memorizing passages that focus on these good things. When bad thoughts pop into your mind, immediately redirect them to God's Word and ask God to change your thought life. This takes great discipline but is very effective.

It is what comes from inside that defiles you. ... All these vile things come from within; they are what defile you.

MARK 7:20-23

Fix your thoughts on what is true, and honorable, and right, and pure, and lovely, and admirable. Think about things that are excellent and worthy of praise.

PHILIPPIANS 4:8

I know, my God, that you examine our hearts and rejoice when you find integrity there.

1 CHRONICLES 29:17

USE TIME WISELY

The Bible is clear that how we use our precious little time on earth will have an impact on our life in heaven. The more time you invest in discovering the purpose for which God created you and in living out that purpose with obedience and responsibility, the more meaningful and significant your time on earth.

The best way to find the time you need is to devote time to God for worship and time to yourself for rest. Devoting time to God gives you spiritual refreshment and the opportunity to discover His priorities for you. Devoting time to rest gives you physical refreshment and the energy to do what you are called to do in the time you have.

Teach us to realize the brevity of life, so that we may grow in wisdom.

PSALM 90:12

"This is what the LORD commanded: Tomorrow will be a day of complete rest, a holy Sabbath day set apart for the LORD. So bake or boil as much as you want today, and set aside what is left for tomorrow."

EXODUS 16:23

For everything there is a season, a time for every activity under heaven. ... God has made everything beautiful for its own time. He has planted eternity in the human heart.

ECCLESIASTES 3:1, 11

TIRED AND WEARY

Being overly tired is dangerous because it can keep you from thinking clearly or cause you to do or say something you'll regret. But when it's impossible to get enough rest, your weariness is an opportunity to experience God's faithfulness. He will give you renewed strength when you grow weary.

When you come to Him in praise, He refreshes your heart. When you come to Him in prayer, He refreshes your soul. When you come to Him in solitude, He refreshes your body. When you come to Him in need, He refreshes your mind. Coming to God releases you from your burdens and allows you to draw strength from Him, the source of strength.

Jesus said, "Come to me, all of you who are weary and carry heavy burdens, and I will give you rest."

MATTHEW 11:28

Be strong in the Lord and in his mighty power.

EPHESIANS 6:10

He gives power to the weak and strength to the powerless. Even youths will become weak and tired, and young men will fall in exhaustion. But those who trust in the LORD will find new strength. They will soar high on wings like eagles. They will run and not grow weary. They will walk and not faint.

ISAIAH 40:29-31

A CHEERFUL GIVER

Tithing is not just a religious law. Tithing is both practical and symbolic. When we tithe, not only are we supporting God's work, fellow believers, and those in need, we are showing our commitment to God and honoring Him for His provision and faithfulness.

A habit of tithing makes God your top priority and gives you the proper perspective on the rest of your paycheck. Instead of asking, "How much of my money do I need to give to God?" ask yourself, "How much of God's money do I need to keep?"

You must each decide in your heart how much to give. And don't give reluctantly or in response to pressure. "For God loves a person who gives cheerfully."

2 CORINTHIANS 9:7

Give, and you will receive. Your gift will return to you in full—pressed down, shaken together to make room for more, running over, and poured into your lap. The amount you give will determine the amount you get back.

LUKE 6:38

MUTUAL TRUST

Mutual trust strengthens and deepens relationships because you know that what others tell you is true and that they are acting in your best interest. When you trust someone, you have peace of mind about that person. You are free to fully enjoy and engage in the relationship.

Trust is vital in your relationships. If you can't trust someone, there is no way you can have a healthy, close relationship. If you don't trust God, the only One who is completely trustworthy, you cannot experience true peace or the ability to enjoy and engage in a relationship with Him. When you learn to trust God, you will never have to question His motives or what He says. You will know that He always has your best interests in mind.

Putting confidence in an unreliable person in times of trouble is like chewing with a broken tooth or walking on a lame foot.

PROVERBS 25:19

Who can find a virtuous and capable wife? She is more precious than rubies. Her husband can trust her, and she will greatly enrich his life.

PROVERBS 31:10-11

Those who know your name trust in you, for you, O LORD, do not abandon those who search for you.

PSALM 9:10

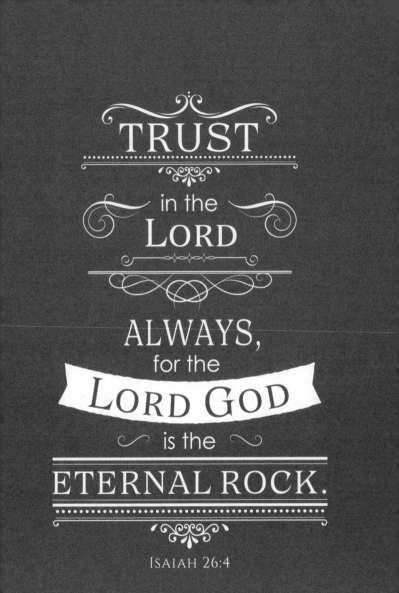

TRUST

in the
LORD

ALWAYS,
for the
LORD GOD

is the

ETERNAL ROCK.

ISAIAH 26:4

GODLY VALUES

You may have heard someone say, "He doesn't have any values." But such a statement is simply not true. Everyone has values, either good or bad. The problem comes when you don't have God's values but instead let the world's values shape you.

Your values are clear to those around you because what you do, how you spend your time and money, and what you talk about show exactly what you value most. When you value God the most, it will be reflected in the words you speak and how you spend your time, energy, and money.

When you love and worship the Lord, obey Him wholeheartedly, trust Him with your future, and serve Him by serving others, you are displaying godly values.

Wherever your treasure is, there the desires of your heart will also be.

LUKE 12:34

"You must always act in the fear of the LORD, with faithfulness and an undivided heart."

2 CHRONICLES 19:9

Who may worship in your sanctuary, LORD? Who may enter your presence on your holy hill? Those who lead blameless lives and do what is right, speaking the truth from sincere hearts.

PSALM 15:1-2

GAIN THE VICTORY

Your greatest victory has already been won by Christ, when you received God's gift of salvation. But you need daily victory over the strongholds of sin that threaten your ability to effectively live the Christian life. Sin destroys—sometimes dramatically, sometimes slowly. Sin harasses you, constantly threatening to draw you away from your relationship with God.

To live a victorious life, you must relentlessly battle against sin and remove it from your heart piece by piece. When you trust Jesus Christ with your life, He equips you with everything you need to conquer sin and gain the victory.

> Put on every piece of God's armor so you will be able to resist the enemy in the time of evil. Then after the battle you will still be standing firm.
>
> EPHESIANS 6:13

> Every child of God defeats this evil world, and we achieve this victory through our faith. And who can win this battle against the world? Only those who believe that Jesus is the Son of God.
>
> 1 JOHN 5:4-5

> Thank God! He gives us victory over sin and death through our Lord Jesus Christ.
>
> 1 CORINTHIANS 15:57

A CLEAR VISION

Having spiritual vision is having God's picture of your future. Here are several ways to fill yourself with God's vision for your life: through the study of His Word, through the conscience He has given you, through the counsel of other believers, and through prayer.

To have better spiritual vision, you need the lens of faith—the ability to believe that there is more to life than what you see, that God is at work and has a place for you in His plan. As you learn to see through the lens of faith, God's vision for you will become clear.

It was by faith that Moses left the land of Egypt, not fearing the king's anger. He kept right on going because he kept his eyes on the one who is invisible.

HEBREWS 11:27

Don't copy the behavior and customs of this world, but let God transform you into a new person by changing the way you think. Then you will learn to know God's will for you, which is good and pleasing and perfect.

ROMANS 12:2

The LORD directs our steps, so why try to understand everything along the way?

PROVERBS 20:24

GOD'S WARNINGS

You can look at warnings as intrusions that prevent you from enjoying life, or you can look at them as blessings that protect you so you can enjoy life more. God's warnings are designed to protect His people from the consequences of foolish actions. For example, God's warning to avoid sexual immorality prevents you from the possibility of a broken heart, an unplanned pregnancy, or a STD.

All too often we view these warnings as obstacles to our freedom. When we do that, we rebel against the very things that are designed to protect us. God's warnings are His way of trying to save you from doing something you'll later regret.

> The laws of the LORD are true; each one is fair. They are more desirable than gold, even the finest gold. They are a warning to your servant, a great reward for those who obey them.
>
> PSALM 19:9-11

> To whom can I give warning? Who will listen when I speak? Their ears are closed, and they cannot hear.
>
> JEREMIAH 6:10

> If you listen to these commands of the LORD your God that I am giving you today, and if you carefully obey them, the LORD will make you the head and not the tail.
>
> DEUTERONOMY 28:13

GAINING WISDOM

The Bible has so much to say about wisdom (the entire book of Proverbs is devoted to it) because successfully navigating through life requires so much of it.

Wisdom helps you recognize that an all-powerful, all-knowing God has designed a moral universe in which there are consequences for your choices, either good or bad. Wisdom begins with understanding your accountability to your Creator and your full dependence on Him. It's not *what* you know but *who* you know. Wisdom from God helps you develop a godly perspective that penetrates the deceptive and distorted messages of this world.

Wisdom is choosing to apply God's truth and principles to your daily relationships and situations. It helps you know the difference between good and bad, right and wrong.

Fear of the LORD is the foundation of wisdom. Knowledge of the Holy One results in good judgment.

PROVERBS 9:10

If you need wisdom, ask our generous God, and he will give it to you. He will not rebuke you for asking.

JAMES 1:5

The wise are mightier than the strong, and those with knowledge grow stronger and stronger.

PROVERBS 24:5

Fear of the LORD is the FOUNDATION of TRUE WISDOM. All who obey his COMMANDMENTS will grow in WISDOM.

PSALM 111:10

POWERFUL WORDS

Our words are like gifts that we give to God or to other people. The things we say and the meaning behind our words have an enormous impact on those who hear them. You wouldn't give an obscene gift to the president of your company, or even to a friend and you certainly wouldn't want to give something insulting to an enemy. Words are no different.

In fact, the greatest gift you can give to others is not in a box covered with paper and bows but in the words you use to encourage, inspire, comfort, and challenge them. Don't let your words be annoying, insulting, demeaning, or simply useless. Your words truly matter because what you say reveals the condition of your heart.

> If you claim to be religious but don't control your tongue, you are fooling yourself, and your religion is worthless.
>
> JAMES 1:26

> Let everything you say be good and helpful, so that your words will be an encouragement to those who hear them.
>
> EPHESIANS 4:29

> May the words of my mouth and the meditation of my heart be pleasing to you, O LORD, my rock and my redeemer.
>
> PSALM 19:14

MEANINGFUL WORK

Work is part of God's plan for our lives, so our work matters to God. Those who work diligently experience many benefits in their own lives and are able to pass them on to others. At its best, work honors God and brings meaning and joy to your life. In your work you should model characteristics of God's work, such as excellence, concern for the well-being of others, purpose, beauty, and service.

Whatever your job, there is immense dignity in all honest human labor because your work is an opportunity to serve God and others. Believe that God has placed you in your position for a reason, and then do your work well until He opens a door of opportunity for you to move on.

Make it your goal to live a quiet life, minding your own business and working with your hands, just as we instructed you before.

1 THESSALONIANS 4:11

Work with enthusiasm, as though you were working for the Lord rather than for people.

EPHESIANS 6:7

Work willingly at whatever you do, as though you were working for the Lord rather than for people. Remember that the Lord will give you an inheritance as your reward.

COLOSSIANS 3:23-24

WORTHY IN GOD'S EYES

Do you get your sense of self-worth from a combination of looks, accomplishments, career, possessions, and social status? This is a precarious way to live. The most secure and lasting place to find worth is in your relationship with God.

It is truly wonderful when you realize just how much God values you! God created you and knew you intimately before you were born. He loved you enough to rescue you from eternal punishment for your sins through Jesus' death and resurrection.

Because of this, you know you have tremendous value and worth in God's eyes. Because of the magnitude of God's forgiveness and grace and His love for you, He is worthy of your praise, gratitude, and love in return.

God created human beings in his own image. In the image of God he created them; male and female he created them.

GENESIS 1:27

You made [people] only a little lower than God and crowned them with glory and honor.

PSALM 8:5

How precious are your thoughts about me, O God.

PSALM 139:17

BREAKING ADDICTION

Sin is the worst addiction. It controls you. As with other addictions, sin often results when you lose your self-control. Ironically, the only way to recover self-control is to let God control you. His control is always for your benefit and for your spiritual growth.

God can break the power of any addiction you are struggling with when you give Him control of your life. Surrender to the Holy Spirit, and God will replace addictive impulses with life-affirming desires. While it is important to seek the help of others, it is only with God's help that you will have the ultimate power to overcome addiction.

You say, "I am allowed to do anything"—but not everything is good for you. And even though "I am allowed to do anything," I must not become a slave to anything.

1 CORINTHIANS 6:12

You belong to God, my dear children. You have already won a victory over those people, because the Spirit who lives in you is greater than the spirit who lives in the world.

1 JOHN 4:4

You are not controlled by your sinful nature. You are controlled by the Spirit if you have the Spirit of God living in you.

ROMANS 8:9

DOES GOD REALLY CARE?

When no one else gives you words of affirmation, you can still feel affirmed because the almighty God chose to create you in His image and longs to be in relationship with you. He sent His own Son to die for your sins so that you could have the opportunity to live with Him forever.

God's words and actions toward you affirm that He desires your heart and soul, and that you matter to Him. When you realize just how passionate God is about you, you can experience a breakthrough in your spiritual life. You will begin to notice all the little ways He interrupts your day with a blessing here and an encouragement there.

The more you see with spiritual eyes the daily evidence of God's love for you, the more confident and affirmed you will feel.

Surely your goodness and unfailing love will pursue me all the days of my life.

PSALM 23:6

The LORD is like a father to his children, tender and compassionate to those who fear him.

PSALM 103:13

May God be merciful and bless us. May his face smile with favor on us.

PSALM 67:1

For the
LORD your God
— is a —
MIGHTY SAVIOR.
He will take delight
in you with
GLADNESS.
With his
LOVE,
he will calm all your fears.
— He will —
REJOICE
over you with
joyful songs.
ZEPHANIAH 3:17

THE DANGER OF APATHY

Ironically, apathy can cause you to lose what you most want. If you are apathetic toward your wife, you are in danger of losing her. If you are apathetic about investing your money, you are in danger of losing your retirement income. If you are apathetic toward God, you are in danger of losing the priceless rewards that await His followers in heaven.

Apathy often seems to be a passive force that simply lulls you to sleep, but it can also be an aggressive force that prevents you from keeping what is most meaningful and important to you.

They have made it an empty wasteland; I hear its mournful cry. The whole land is desolate, and no one even cares.

JEREMIAH 12:11

What makes us think we can escape if we ignore this great salvation that was first announced by the Lord Jesus himself and then delivered to us by those who heard him speak?

HEBREWS 2:3

Watch out that you do not lose what we have worked so hard to achieve. Be diligent so that you receive your full reward.

2 JOHN 1:8

THE POWER OF AN APOLOGY

Saying "I'm sorry" for something you have done wrong is one of the most difficult things to do. You have to recognize your fault, face it head-on, and then humble yourself enough to admit it to someone else.

A sincere apology is the first step in changing your behavior and committing to do the right thing. Refusing to apologize when you know you're wrong is a clear sign of pride, which can have devastating effects on your life and relationships. But being willing to apologize demonstrates humility and opens the door to healing and blessing.

If you need a breakthrough in your relationship with a coworker, a loved one, or God Himself, the practice of admitting when you are wrong will help you reach a new level of trust and respect.

The Holy One, says this: "I live in the high and holy place with those whose spirits are contrite and humble. I restore the crushed spirit of the humble and revive the courage of those with repentant hearts."

ISAIAH 57:15

People who conceal their sins will not prosper, but if they confess and turn from them, they will receive mercy. Blessed are those who fear to do wrong, but the stubborn are headed for serious trouble.

PROVERBS 28:13-14

THE ANTIDOTE TO BOREDOM

The dictionary defines boredom as being weary with tedious dullness. It might come from doing the same thing over and over or doing work with no apparent purpose or doing nothing for too long. Boredom is dangerous because it signifies lack of purpose and passion for anything meaningful.

The antidote to boredom is finding something purposeful and significant to do. God has a purpose for you, and finding that purpose is a revelation. From that time on, you will never be bored! Start by volunteering in a ministry at your local church, or find a hobby that helps you develop a skill. Then you will have something to look forward to each day. The fire of passionate living will ignite in your heart, and other people will be attracted to your enthusiasm.

Imitate God, therefore, in everything you do. Live a life filled with love, following the example of Christ.

EPHESIANS 5:1-2

Don't look out only for your own interests, but take an interest in others, too.

PHILIPPIANS 2:4

Let's not get tired of doing what is good. At just the right time we will reap a harvest of blessing if we don't give up.

GALATIANS 6:9

SUCCESSFUL IN BUSINESS

God endorses hard work, ingenuity, fair business practices, and success. Paul, Aquila, and Priscilla were Christian leaders in both ministry and business and managed to do well at balancing both.

The quality of your work and your enthusiasm for it reveal the nature of your commitment to Christ. Hard work done with excellence and integrity honors God and may bring material resources that can be used for God's glory.

But hard work does not always lead to material success. What is most important is that you do your work as though God were your boss. If you work to serve Him, you will be successful in God's eyes.

Do not defraud or rob your neighbor. Do not make your hired workers wait until the next day to receive their pay.

LEVITICUS 19:13

A Jew named Aquila ... had recently arrived from Italy with his wife, Priscilla. ... Paul lived and worked with them, for they were tentmakers just as he was.

ACTS 18:1-3

Commit your actions to the LORD, and your plans will succeed.

PROVERBS 16:3

STRIKE A BALANCE

We often operate under the false assumption that being busy means being productive or that resting means being lazy. But it's possible to have unproductive activity and productive rest!

The Bible points out many benefits of being busy, such as earning a living, providing for your family, and advancing God's kingdom. But being too busy can damage your relationships (with God and with others), cause burnout, or prevent you from focusing on your real priorities. As with anything you do, learning to strike a balance between working, having fun, and resting will allow you to be productive in all areas of life.

We are merely moving shadows, and all our busy rushing ends in nothing. We heap up wealth, not knowing who will spend it.

PSALM 39:6

Enthusiasm without knowledge is no good; haste makes mistakes.

PROVERBS 19:2

Jesus said, "Come to me, all of you who are weary and carry heavy burdens, and I will give you rest. Take my yoke upon you. Let me teach you, because I am humble and gentle at heart, and you will find rest for your souls."

MATTHEW 11:28-29

Seek the **KINGDOM OF GOD** above all else & **LIVE RIGHTEOUSLY,** and he will give you **EVERYTHING** you need.

MATTHEW 6:33

A CHANGE FOR GOOD

Change is one of the great constants of life. Some changes are positive: making a new friend, moving into a new house, receiving a financial windfall. Other changes are negative: suffering a tragic loss, getting laid off from a job, surviving the upheaval of a natural disaster. Either way, change is stressful.

The Bible offers two truths about change. The first is that despite the changing world around us, God is changeless and dependable. The second is that God wants an inner change of heart, called repentance, that produces an outward change of lifestyle, called obedience. When you change your heart, you will change your life forever.

Don't copy the behavior and customs of this world, but let God transform you into a new person by changing the way you think. Then you will learn to know God's will for you, which is good and pleasing and perfect.

ROMANS 12:2

Now repent of your sins and turn to God, so that your sins may be wiped away.

ACTS 3:19

I am certain that God, who began the good work within you, will continue his work until it is finally finished on the day when Christ Jesus returns.

PHILIPPIANS 1:6

MEETING TOGETHER

Together all believers make up God's family, and it is only by meeting together that you can bond. One purpose of the church is to equip God's people to do God's work and to encourage them in their faith. The church is where Christians learn to work together in unity, reconciling differences among themselves in a way that is only possible through Christ and His Spirit.

When you meet together with other believers, you build each other up and help each other. The church needs you because the body of Christ is not complete unless you are there.

The church is his body; it is made full and complete by Christ, who fills all things everywhere with himself.

EPHESIANS 1:23

The human body has many parts, but the many parts make up one whole body. So it is with the body of Christ.

1 CORINTHIANS 12:12

Let us not neglect our meeting together, as some people do, but encourage one another, especially now that the day of his return is drawing near.

HEBREWS 10:25

HEARING GOD'S VOICE

The best way to be certain you are hearing God's voice is to know God. Prayer is talking to God and building a relationship with Him. Good conversation also includes listening, so you must allow God to speak to you. Only when you hear God can He make His wisdom and resources available to you.

Just as a piano is tuned using a standard tuning fork, so you can only get in tune with God by comparing yourself to the unchanging standards for living found in the Bible. As God communicates to you through His Word, you will begin to hear or discern just what He wants of you. As your spiritual hearing is fine-tuned, you will become a better listener, better able to hear God when He calls you to a certain task that He has reserved just for you.

My sheep listen to my voice; I know them, and they follow me.

JOHN 10:27

Anyone who belongs to God listens gladly to the words of God.

JOHN 8:47

Don't worry about anything; instead, pray about everything. Tell God what you need, and thank him for all he has done. Then you will experience God's peace.

PHILIPPIANS 4:6-7

NO COMPROMISE

There is a time to compromise and a time to stand firm. When the forces of evil tempt you to give up your convictions, you cannot budge.

To compromise God's truth, God's ways, or God's Word is to negotiate with that which is unholy. The test of acceptable compromise is simple: Can you reach an agreement that satisfies both parties without sacrificing anyone's morals? If you give up godliness in exchange for anything else, it's a bad bargain. You lose and Satan wins. You can experience a divine moment if you refuse to compromise your convictions, and you will feel a sense of peace that you have done the right thing.

> Daniel was determined not to defile himself by eating the food and wine given to them by the king. He asked the chief of staff for permission not to eat these unacceptable foods.
>
> DANIEL 1:8

> Be very careful never to make a treaty with the people who live in the land where you are going. If you do, you will follow their evil ways and be trapped.
>
> EXODUS 34:12

> Put on all of God's armor so that you will be able to stand firm against all strategies of the devil.
>
> EPHESIANS 6:11

ADMIT YOUR GUILT

Confession is admitting to other people or to God that you are guilty of some wrong. When you have to acknowledge the ugliness of your own sin, it can be embarrassing and even painful.

But confession is a necessary part of knowing God, receiving His forgiveness, being released from guilt, and finding a new start. Confession is essential to knowing God because it is only through humility that you can establish honesty and trust with Him.

Confession is essential to being freed from the eternal consequences of sin because it brings about God's forgiveness.

Finally, I confessed all my sins to you and stopped trying to hide my guilt. I said to myself, "I will confess my rebellion to the LORD." And you forgave me! All my guilt is gone.

PSALM 32:5

If we confess our sins to him, he is faithful and just to forgive us our sins and to cleanse us from all wickedness.

1 JOHN 1:9

Confess your sins to each other and pray for each other so that you may be healed. The earnest prayer of a righteous person has great power and produces wonderful results.

JAMES 5:16

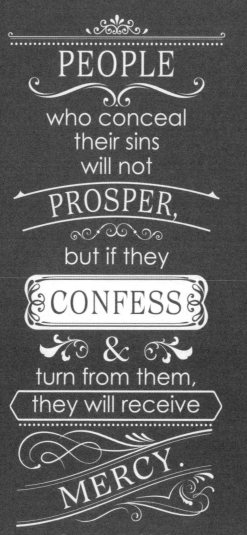

PEOPLE
who conceal
their sins
will not
PROSPER,
but if they
CONFESS
&
turn from them,
they will receive
MERCY.

PROVERBS 28:13

HANDLING CONFLICT

The Bible does not hide from the issue of conflict, and it does not condemn all conflict as sinful. From Moses to David to Jesus to Paul, all of the Bible's greatest figures found themselves in conflict. Disagreements happen. But the manner in which conflicts are resolved is extremely important.

Conflict can become the catalyst for developing greater understanding, intimacy, and depth in your relationships, or it can cause anger, bitterness, and broken relationships. With the Holy Spirit's help, you will learn to turn arguments into peace, anger into patience, rage into gentleness, and sinful thoughts and actions into self-control.

The Holy Spirit produces this kind of fruit in our lives: love, joy, peace, patience, kindness, goodness, faithfulness, gentleness, and self-control.

GALATIANS 5:22-23

You have heard the law that says, "Love your neighbor" and hate your enemy. But I say, love your enemies! Pray for those who persecute you! In that way, you will be acting as true children of your Father in heaven.

MATTHEW 5:43-45

God blesses those who work for peace, for they will be called the children of God.

MATTHEW 5:9

BE COURAGEOUS

The early church was constantly threatened with persecution. The believers did not pray for the threats to be taken away but for the courage to face them. Sometimes God will remove the things that frighten you. But more often the Holy Spirit gives you the boldness to turn those fears into opportunities for spiritual growth and sharing your faith.

If God were to take away everything that frightens you, there would be no need for hope in your life. It is hope that helps you see beyond your immediate crisis and place your current problem, as well as your eternal future, in God's hands. When you are overwhelmed by the enormity of the problem facing you, let it be a time to recognize that God is right by your side.

All the believers lifted their voices together in prayer to God: "O Lord, hear their threats, and give us, your servants, great boldness. Stretch out your hand with healing power; may miraculous signs and wonders be done through the name of your holy servant Jesus." After this prayer, the meeting place shook, and they were all filled with the Holy Spirit. Then they preached the word of God with boldness.

ACTS 4:24, 29-31

Be strong and courageous! Do not be afraid or discouraged. For the LORD your God is with you wherever you go.

JOSHUA 1:9

THE DARKNESS OF DEPRESSION

God does not regard depression as sin, nor does He take it lightly. Rather, He responds with great tenderness, understanding, and compassion to those who suffer the darkness of depression.

When you are depressed, the Bible helps you recognize the lies of Satan, the temptations that might come your way, and the ways the devil fuels your depression by distracting you from God's promises and power.

As you become more aware of these things, your perspective will begin to change. Develop the habit of seeking God and counting on His Word to be true; then you will discover the encouragement you need.

I have told you these things so that you will be filled with my joy. Yes, your joy will overflow!

JOHN 15:11

Those who listen to instruction will prosper; those who trust the LORD will be joyful.

PROVERBS 16:20

Even when I walk through the darkest valley, I will not be afraid, for you are close beside me. Your rod and your staff protect and comfort me.

PSALM 23:4

BE DISCERNING

The Bible tells us that discernment is necessary to mature in your faith. In fact, it says that recognizing the difference between right and wrong is a developed skill. When you grow and mature in your faith, you will be able to recognize temptation before it overcomes you. You will learn to distinguish between truth and lies, between God's voice and other voices.

When you know the Scriptures, you will be able to discern false teaching or if someone is using a passage of Scripture incorrectly. When you practice discernment and train yourself to detect right from wrong, you will be able to avoid the pitfalls and confusion that so many people fall into.

> You need someone to teach you again the basic things about God's word. You are like babies who need milk and cannot eat solid food. For someone who lives on milk is still an infant and doesn't know how to do what is right. Solid food is for those who are mature, who through training have the skill to recognize the difference between right and wrong.
>
> HEBREWS 5:12-14

> Give me understanding and I will obey your instructions; I will put them into practice with all my heart.
>
> PSALM 119:34

OPEN TO GOD'S CORRECTION

Like Jerusalem at the time of Zephaniah, you can stubbornly refuse to listen to God—or anyone else—and ignore the correction that could help you. When you get to that point, you are rebelling against God, and He may use adversity to get your attention and discipline you.

Stay open to God's correction in your life, follow His directions for living found in the Bible, and listen carefully to the advice of godly people whom you respect. Be careful, however, not to immediately assume that your troubles (or the troubles someone else is experiencing) are the result of God's discipline. If you have been sincerely trying to follow God, chances are that there is another reason for your adversity.

My child, don't reject the LORD's discipline. For the LORD corrects those he loves.

PROVERBS 3:11-12

No one can tell [Jerusalem] anything; it refuses all correction. It does not trust in the LORD or draw near to its God.

ZEPHANIAH 3:2

Joyful are those you discipline, LORD.

PSALM 94:12

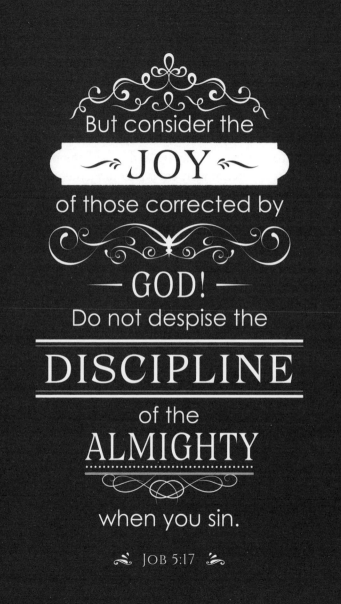

But consider the

JOY

of those corrected by

— GOD! —

Do not despise the

DISCIPLINE

of the

ALMIGHTY

when you sin.

JOB 5:17

FEELING DISCOURAGED

When you are discouraged, you feel like giving up—on God, friends, family, career, even hope itself. When you reach your lowest point, you must decide whether you will sink deeper into the mire or begin to climb your way up and out of the pit. The opposite of discouragement is encouragement, and it is the antidote you need when you are down.

God is your greatest encourager. He never abandons you, and He heals your wounds. He inspires you with His Word; He listens to your prayers and answers them; He revives you with hope. When you feel discouraged, seek God's help first. Then find encouragement from others who can help you put things in perspective. Face head-on the cause of your discouragement, and plan steps to recover. When you see a way out, your hope will return, and over time so will your joy.

Why am I discouraged? Why is my heart so sad? I will put my hope in God! I will praise him again—my Savior and my God! Now I am deeply discouraged, but I will remember you. … Each day the LORD pours his unfailing love upon me, and through each night I sing his songs, praying to God who gives me life.

PSALM 42:5-8

From the depths of despair, O LORD, I call for your help.

PSALM 130:1

FILLING THE EMPTINESS

Many things can cause you to feel empty—the death of a loved one, the end of a friendship, being ignored or rejected. These feelings of emptiness all have one thing in common: some kind of loss. Loss empties your emotional tank and uses up all your reserves. It leaves you hungry and thirsty, looking for something to fill and satisfy the emptiness.

This is the moment Satan's been waiting for. He tries to deceive you into thinking that what he offers can satisfy you. But only God can fill the emptiness inside you and satisfy your deepest needs. When your heart is filled with the love, truth, and goodness of God, there is no room for evil to enter.

It is only through the presence of God's Spirit within you that meaning, purpose, and satisfaction will be restored.

May you experience the love of Christ, though it is too great to understand fully. Then you will be made complete with all the fullness of life and power that comes from God.

EPHESIANS 3:19

Jesus replied, "Anyone who drinks this water will soon become thirsty again. But those who drink the water I give will never be thirsty again. It becomes a fresh, bubbling spring within them, giving them eternal life."

JOHN 4:13-14

FINISHING WELL

Life is like a marathon. The greatest reward for finishing well is the prize of eternal life with God. Just as marathoners must train hard to build up their endurance so they can run the race and finish well, so Christians must train to build up endurance for living a life of faith in Jesus and staying strong to the end. When you have built up your endurance, you will not collapse during the race but will be able to push on toward the goal of becoming more and more like Jesus.

Finally, you cross the finish line into heaven and receive the eternal rewards God has promised. You can strengthen your endurance by focusing on God's promises for the future instead of the problems of the moment.

Let's not get tired of doing what is good. At just the right time we will reap a harvest of blessing if we don't give up.

GALATIANS 6:9

If we endure hardship, we will reign with him. If we deny him, he will deny us.

2 TIMOTHY 2:12

When troubles come your way, consider it an opportunity for great joy. For you know that when your faith is tested, your endurance has a chance to grow.

JAMES 1:2-3

ETERNAL REWARDS

If the rewards of this earthly life were all we had to live for, then a "why bother" attitude might be appropriate. But there are two reasons why this perspective is wrong: First, when you try to obey God, you put yourself in a position to enjoy life the way it is meant to be enjoyed; your relationships are faithful, your life has integrity, and your conscience is clear.

Second, this life is not all there is. The Bible is clear that those who trust in Jesus Christ and turn to Him for forgiveness receive the promise of eternal life. Your faithfulness in this life may or may not result in material prosperity, but the eternal rewards of heaven will be greater than you could ever imagine.

> God has made everything beautiful for its own time. He has planted eternity in the human heart, but even so, people cannot see the whole scope of God's work from beginning to end.
>
> ECCLESIASTES 3:11

> No eye has seen, no ear has heard, and no mind has imagined what God has prepared for those who love him.
>
> 1 CORINTHIANS 2:9

> I am the resurrection and the life. Anyone who believes in me will live, even after dying.
>
> JOHN 11:25

A HEALTHY FEAR

Because God is so great and mighty, and because He holds the power of life and death in His hands, you should have a healthy, reverent fear of Him.

When you have a healthy fear of God, you recognize what He could do if He gave you what you deserve. A healthy fear should drive you to God for forgiveness. You can also rejoice that instead of punishment, God gives you mercy and forgiveness. He even desires to have a relationship with you.

Fearing God is not the same as being afraid of Him. Fearing God means being awed by His power and goodness. This draws you closer to Him and the blessings He gives.

Doesn't his majesty terrify you? Doesn't your fear of him overwhelm you?

JOB 13:11

Let the whole world fear the LORD, and let everyone stand in awe of him.

PSALM 33:8

Fear of the LORD is the foundation of wisdom.

PROVERBS 9:10

Serve the LORD with reverent fear, and rejoice with trembling.

PSALM 2:11

Here now is my
final conclusion:

FEAR GOD

&

— OBEY —

his commands,
for this is

EVERYONE'S

DUTY.

ECCLESIASTES 12:13

A GENEROUS GIVER

It's not what you have but what you do with what you have that's significant—whether it's money, time, or talents.

Generosity is an important character trait in God's eyes because it is the opposite of selfishness. Selfishness promotes greed, stinginess, envy, and hardheartedness—all traits that destroy relationships.

Generosity promotes giving, trust, mercy, and putting the needs of others above your own—all traits that build relationships. And true generosity involves sacrifice, which is the key to changing stinginess into selflessness. When you realize that everything you have is a gift from our generous God, you will be motivated to share your material resources and earthly possessions more freely.

Don't forget to do good and to share with those in need. These are the sacrifices that please God.

HEBREWS 13:16

You must each decide in your heart how much to give. And don't give reluctantly or in response to pressure. "For God loves a person who gives cheerfully."

2 CORINTHIANS 9:7

Remember the words of the Lord Jesus: "It is more blessed to give than to receive."

ACTS 20:35

TRUE GREATNESS

God warns against pretending to be something we're not, especially if we're pretending to be spiritually great. There's a difference between wanting to be a part of God's great work and wanting to achieve personal greatness through doing God's work. If you're not sure which side you're on, examine your motives. If the greatest benefactor of your achievements is yourself, then perhaps you are trying to find greatness in the wrong way.

True greatness comes from knowing your real value in God's eyes and being honest with yourself and others. It is better to be honest about your failures than to lie about your successes. That is why humility is necessary for true greatness. Don't be fooled into striving to gain everything you desire in this world at the cost of your eternal rewards in heaven.

Let's build a great city for ourselves with a tower that reaches into the sky. This will make us famous.

GENESIS 11:4

Jesus said to his disciples, "If any of you wants to be my follower, you must turn from your selfish ways, take up your cross, and follow me."

MATTHEW 16:24

Whoever wants to be first must take last place and be the servant of everyone else.

MARK 9:35

THE HAND OF GOD

Maybe you think that God's work on this earth comes only in the form of dramatic miracles, like raising someone from the dead. But all around you are supernatural occurrences from the hand of God. They may not be as dramatic as the parting of the Red Sea, but they are no less powerful.

Think of the birth of a baby, the healing of an illness, the rebirth of the earth in spring, the restoration of broken relationships through the work of love and forgiveness, the salvation of sinners through faith alone, the specific call of God in your life. These are just a few ways God acts in His creation.

If you think you've never seen the hand of God at work, look closer. He is active all around you.

Who can list the glorious miracles of the LORD? Who can ever praise him enough?

PSALM 106:2

"Yes," says the LORD, "I will do mighty miracles for you, like those I did when I rescued you from slavery in Egypt."

MICAH 7:15

Seek his will in all you do, and he will show you which path to take.

PROVERBS 3:6

ACCEPTING HELP

All of us have limitations. Sometimes we need help. That's why God created us to be in relationship with other people. We need help to get work done. We need help to restore a relationship. We need help to develop our skills. We need help thinking through a problem. We need help to say, "I'm sorry."

God wants to help you, too. He is your ultimate helper, for He is wiser, stronger, and more loving than any person you know. Cultivate the habit of seeking help from God and from others and offer help to those in need. You will experience great joy when God comes to your rescue, and you may pass that joy on to others when they see God helping them through you.

Whenever they were in trouble and turned to the LORD, the God of Israel, and sought him out, they found him.

2 CHRONICLES 15:4

If someone has enough money to live well and sees a brother or sister in need but shows no compassion—how can God's love be in that person?

1 JOHN 3:17

Two people are better off than one, for they can help each other succeed. If one person falls, the other can reach out and help.

ECCLESIASTES 4:9-10

GOD OF THE IMPOSSIBLE

Learn to recognize and appreciate the "impossible" things God accomplishes for you and around you each day: the gift of forgiveness, the change of seasons, the intricacies of the human body and its ability to heal, the exact conditions needed to support life on this earth, the birth of a baby.

The more you see the impossible acts of God with eyes of faith, the stronger your faith in God will become. There should be no doubt that God specializes in doing what from a human perspective is impossible. But the end of your abilities is the beginning of His. The God who spoke all creation into being can do the impossible for you.

Simply believe that He can—and that He wants to.

Those who heard this said, "Then who in the world can be saved?" He replied, "What is impossible for people is possible with God."

LUKE 18:26-27

This is what the LORD of Heaven's Armies says: All this may seem impossible to you now. But is it impossible for me? says the LORD of Heaven's Armies.

ZECHARIAH 8:6

Now all glory to God, who is able, through his mighty power at work within us, to accomplish infinitely more than we might ask or think.

EPHESIANS 3:20

I AM
the LORD,
THE GOD
of all the
PEOPLES
of the world.
Is anything
TOO HARD
FOR ME?

··· JEREMIAH 32:27 ···

A MAN OF INTEGRITY

Integrity is essentially how well your character corresponds to the character of God. Integrity allows you to enjoy fellowship with God and helps you live under His protection and guidance.

Developing integrity is a process. Just as gold is made pure through a refining process that tests the metal with fire, so you are made pure through the refining process of gaining integrity. God uses the everyday trials and circumstances of your life to test you and see how pure you are.

If the Lord finds that your heart and actions are becoming increasingly pure through this testing, then your character is becoming more like His, and you are gradually gaining integrity.

The LORD has told you what is good, and this is what he requires of you: to do what is right, to love mercy, and to walk humbly with your God.

MICAH 6:8

"Job is blameless—a man of complete integrity. He fears God and stays away from evil. And he has maintained his integrity, even though you urged me to harm him without cause."

JOB 2:3

Who may worship in your sanctuary, LORD? Those who lead blameless lives and do what is right, speaking the truth from sincere hearts.

PSALM 15:1

GOD IS MERCIFUL

God's mercy gives us a second chance even when we don't deserve it. God's amazing love for us is the reason He is so merciful. God chooses to show mercy to those He loves and who love Him. Even though our sin and rebellion against God deserve His punishment; He offers us forgiveness and eternal life instead.

When you understand that you don't deserve God's mercy but He gives it to you anyway, then you will experience the full impact of God's love for you. Only then will you be able to truly love others and show them mercy, even when they don't deserve it. The mercy you show them will be a reflection of God's unconditional love.

The LORD is compassionate and merciful, slow to get angry and filled with unfailing love. He will not constantly accuse us, nor remain angry forever. He does not punish us for all our sins; he does not deal harshly with us, as we deserve.

PSALM 103:8-10

When God our Savior revealed his kindness and love, he saved us, not because of the righteous things we had done, but because of his mercy. He washed away our sins, giving us a new birth and new life through the Holy Spirit. He generously poured out the Spirit upon us through Jesus Christ our Savior.

TITUS 3:4-6

OBEDIENCE BRINGS JOY

Even though God's commandments are sometimes difficult to obey or don't always make sense from our human perspective, obedience to Him will always bring blessing, joy, and peace. When you look at obedience this way, then you will obey God out of love and gratitude for all He's trying to do for you rather than out of fear of being punished.

The more you obey out of love, the more you will want to obey, and the more obedience will become a lifestyle rather than a chore. Since God is the creator of life, He knows how life is supposed to work. Obedience to His ways demonstrates your trust that God's way is best and that it will work for you.

Obey me, and I will be your God, and you will be my people. Do everything as I say, and all will be well!

JEREMIAH 7:23

If you look carefully into the perfect law that sets you free, and if you do what it says and don't forget what you heard, then God will bless you for doing it.

JAMES 1:25

Oh, the joys of those who do not follow the advice of the wicked, or stand around with sinners, or join in with mockers. But they delight in the law of the LORD, meditating on it day and night.

PSALM 1:1-2

A HAPPY ENDING

Trusting God does not produce a storybook life in which every problem is quickly resolved. Sometimes people get sick and don't get better; relationships break down and can't be restored; jobs are lost and not regained. You can rejoice, however, that you are assured of a happy ending.

When Jesus returns, discomfort, disappointment, disease, pain, and death will disappear, and you will live with joy in God's presence forever. Because this happy ending is utterly certain, you can endure the unanswered questions and unending crises of this life.

Sometimes it's hard to see God in the pain of the present. When you go through times like that, look forward to God's promise of an eternally pain-free future. It will give you a powerful dose of hope to help you through the present.

> God himself will be with them. He will wipe every tear from their eyes, and there will be no more death or sorrow or crying or pain. All these things are gone forever.
>
> REVELATION 21:3-4

> You have turned my mourning into joyful dancing. You have taken away my clothes of mourning and clothed me with joy, that I might sing praises to you and not be silent.
>
> PSALM 30:11-12

FULLY COMMITTED TO GOD

Like all relationships, your relationship with God takes effort and energy. God is always fully committed to you. For your relationship with God to be exciting, you must be fully committed to Him.

Be diligent in your efforts to get to know Him better. Here are three strategies for doing that: Consistently study God's Word, cultivate a thankful heart, and engage in acts of service to others. This will help fight off feelings of apathy toward God and renew your passion for the purpose He has for your life. You will again be excited about the blessings He has given you and has promised you in the future.

You must continue to believe this truth and stand firmly in it. Don't drift away from the assurance you received when you heard the Good News. The Good News has been preached all over the world, and I, Paul, have been appointed as God's servant to proclaim it.

COLOSSIANS 1:23

I have this complaint against you. You don't love me or each other as you did at first!

REVELATION 2:4

I will give them singleness of heart and put a new spirit within them. I will take away their stony, stubborn heart and give them a tender, responsive heart.

EZEKIEL 11:19

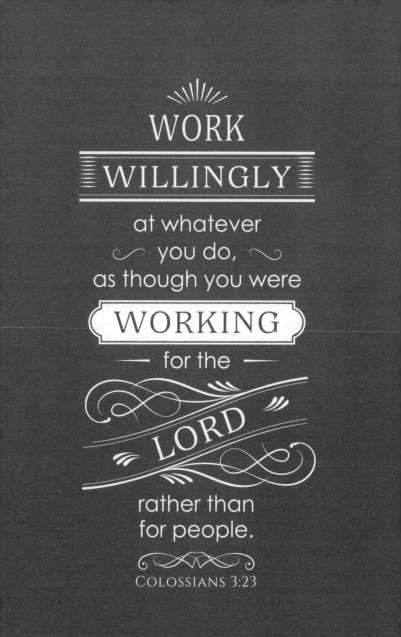

WORK

WILLINGLY

at whatever
you do,
as though you were

WORKING

— for the —

LORD

rather than
for people.

COLOSSIANS 3:23

UNDER PRESSURE

The pressures in your life can be positive or negative. We generally think of peer pressure as a negative influence, such as when you are swayed by friends or coworkers to join them in behavior that is contrary to God's standards for living.

But pressure can be positive, too. For example, the pressure of accountability can be a powerful force for positive change. Jesus reminds us that we are all accountable for our words and actions.

The day is coming when God will judge everything and everyone, and we will receive the good or bad consequences that our actions deserve. This knowledge leads us to renew our commitment to holy living and to seek the forgiveness that only Jesus can offer.

We are pressed on every side by troubles, but we are not crushed. We are perplexed, but not driven to despair. We are hunted down, but never abandoned by God. We get knocked down, but we are not destroyed. Through suffering, our bodies continue to share in the death of Jesus so that the life of Jesus may also be seen in our bodies.

2 CORINTHIANS 4:8-10

Oh, the joys of those who do not follow the advice of the wicked, or stand around with sinners, or join in with mockers.

PSALM 1:1

THE PROMISES OF GOD

God promises salvation to all who accept it. Those who believe that Jesus died for their sins, confess those sins, and are truly sorry for them, will be saved from the punishment their sins deserve. God promises to be with you forever in the form of the Holy Spirit. He promises to forgive you whenever you do wrong, if you just ask Him. He promises that nothing you do is beyond His forgiveness. God promises you peace of heart and mind when you entrust your life to Him. God promises to use even the bad things that happen to you for good purposes.

God promises that Jesus is coming back to judge the world for its deeds. God promises an eternal home in heaven for all who trust in Jesus Christ and acknowledge Him as their Lord.

God loved the world so much that he gave his one and only Son, so that everyone who believes in him will not perish but have eternal life.

JOHN 3:16

We know that God causes everything to work together for the good of those who love God and are called according to his purpose for them.

ROMANS 8:28

Deep in your hearts you know that every promise of the LORD your God has come true. Not a single one has failed!

JOSHUA 23:14

A LEGACY OF FAITH

Remembering the past is an essential part of living in the present and the future. Life is a long journey; to live it to the full, you can't afford to forget some of the important lessons you've learned along the way.

If you do forget, you're likely to repeat your mistakes. One way to remember important milestones and lessons of the past is to establish celebrations, anniversaries, or special times to pause and reflect on where you've been, who has helped you, and what God has done in your life. Try to remember the good and learn from the bad. Never forget what God has done for you. Talk about God's faithfulness—both in your life and in the lives of others—with your friends, family, children, and grandchildren so that you build a legacy of faith for future generations to remember.

You must commit yourselves wholeheartedly to these commands that I am giving you today. Repeat them again and again to your children. Talk about them when you are at home ...

DEUTERONOMY 6:6-7

I will teach you hidden lessons from our past— stories we have heard and known, stories our ancestors handed down to us. We will not hide these truths from our children; we will tell the next generation about the glorious deeds of the LORD, about his power and his mighty wonders.

PSALM 78:2-4

INTIMACY WITHIN MARRIAGE

Here is a strange thought—God likes sex! God created sex. He made men and women as sexual beings to procreate, to populate the next generation, and to express love and delight in each another.

Think of it: He could have created us to reproduce by spores that float through the air, but instead he made sex a source of great enjoyment. God created sex for emotional and physical unity between a man and a woman in marriage. It is also a picture of the unity and intimacy a believer can have with God. Those who enjoy sex within the boundaries created by God will find fulfillment in their marriage, and they will better understand the importance of true intimacy with God.

This explains why a man leaves his father and mother and is joined to his wife, and the two are united into one.

GENESIS 2:24

Each man should have his own wife, and each woman should have her own husband. The husband should fulfill his wife's sexual needs, and the wife should fulfill her husband's needs.

1 CORINTHIANS 7:2-3

You can't say that our bodies were made for sexual immorality. They were made for the Lord, and the Lord cares about our bodies.

1 CORINTHIANS 6:13

GOD CAN'T LIE

You only trust someone who is dependable, who can always be counted on to tell the truth. God didn't just create truth; He *is* truth.

Therefore, God cannot lie. You must believe that in order to believe this: Because God cannot lie, everything He says in the Bible is true. Keep reading through the Bible. Find God's promises to you. Discover how much He loves you and wants a close relationship with you.

When you trust Him with your whole heart, He will make himself known to you in amazing and powerful ways and you will experience a breakthrough in your relationship with Him.

Whatever is good and perfect comes down to us from God our Father, who created all the lights in the heavens. He never changes or casts a shifting shadow. He chose to give birth to us by giving us his true word.

JAMES 1:17-18

God is not a man, so he does not lie. He is not human, so he does not change his mind. Has he ever spoken and failed to act? Has he ever promised and not carried it through?

NUMBERS 23:19

We have received God's Spirit (not the world's spirit), so we can know the wonderful things God has freely given us.

1 CORINTHIANS 2:12

WORTHY OF WORSHIP

The Bible teaches that God alone is worthy of our worship. True worship, then, is the recognition of who God is and of who you are in relation to Him.

Ultimately, everything you do should be based on what you think of the almighty God and how you worship Him. If you aren't giving honor to God, then you are worshiping someone or something else. More than anything else, worship will connect you with God, your only source of lasting hope and joy.

Yours, O LORD, is the greatness, the power, the glory, the victory, and the majesty. Everything in the heavens and on earth is yours, O LORD, and this is your kingdom. We adore you as the one who is over all things.

1 CHRONICLES 29:11

Oh, how great are God's riches and wisdom and knowledge! How impossible it is for us to understand his decisions and his ways!

ROMANS 11:33-34

Therefore, God elevated him to the place of highest honor and gave him the name above all other names, that at the name of Jesus every knee should bow, in heaven and on earth and under the earth, and every tongue confess that Jesus Christ is Lord, to the glory of God the Father.

PHILIPPIANS 2:9-11

A final word:

BE STRONG

IN THE LORD

&

in his

MIGHTY

POWER.

Ephesians 6:10

HONOR the LORD for the GLORY of his name. WORSHIP the LORD in the splendor of his HOLINESS.

PSALM 29:2